Discover the Horizon

Nautical Encyclopedia for Children

Adi Elazari

Dedicated with love,

To my wonderful dear children,
Agam Shoshan,
Maayan Stella
and Peleg Yosef.
This book was written especially for you and inspired by you.

To my dear partner Hai Haim, who sails with me together during
calm and stormy days alike, throughout life's journey.

To my dear mom and dad, Zelig and Batya Landesman,
thanks to your loving support I'm able to sail far and wide.

Voyage Route:

- Port 1 - Haifa, Israel - 34°59'E
- Port 2 – Limassol, Cyprus - 33°42'E
- Port 3 – Izmir, Turkey - 29°55'E
- Port 4 – Piraeus, Greece - 23°38'E
- Port 5 – Thessaloniki, Greece - 22°56'E
- Port 6 – Napoli, Italy - 14°18'E
- Port 7 – Barcelona, Spain 2°10'E
- Port 8 – Gibraltar, UKOTs - 5°21'W
- Port 9 – New York, USA - 73°56'W5°21'W
- Port 10 – Hamilton, Bermuda - 64°46'W
- Port 11 – Papeete, Tahiti - 149°27'W
- Port 12 – Hong Kong, China - 114°10'E
- Port 13 – Alaska, U.S.A. - 150°W'
- Port 14 – Amsterdam, Holland - 4°53'E
- Port 15 – Gibraltar, UKOTs - 5°21'W
- Port 16 – Haifa, Israel - 34°59'E

Port 1 - Haifa, Israel – 34°59'E

It was my first day on the **container ship Ocean 16**, my first bridge shift. We were about to set a sail on an around-the-world cruise, scheduled for three and a half months, one hundred and five days, in twenty-five different countries. I was headed towards seventeen consecutive sailing days at sea across the Pacific Ocean and was excited as I had never been before.

I grabbed the telegraph and started to push it forward. The ship's propellers started to turn at my command, and with them, the entire communication system came to life. An array of commands and instructions traveled back and forth, from the voices of various deck officers.

Telegraph

I couldn't believe it.
Since I was thirteen,
I had dreamt of sailing away,
far from the land and around the world...
and now, here I was.

"All Aboard!"

a small voice suddenly peeped from the control panels.

"Huh?"

Around-the-world-cruise

"Finally, your dream has come true, Adi."

Splashes of salt began flying around the navigational equipment on the bridge console.

"Adi, the only female naval officer in the Israeli Merchant Navy, already eight miles away from shore, on her way to the great sea, while this gigantic ship is entirely under her command - can you believe it?!"

A small creature, that looked like a pirate in a colourful cloak, appeared from in between the different navigation aids panel.

"What... what... who are you?" I leaped back.

"**Ah, I am Eddie, your able seaman**, so pleased to meet you, and at your command!

I have accompanied you during your long years of nautical studies, without you knowing anything about me. I was allowed to reveal myself only on your first cruise as an officer. This is my first voyage too, but no worries, I know everything about seas and cruises, trust me," he said and held out his little hand.

I smiled and shook it.

And so, we set off, me - Third Mate Navigation Officer Adi, and Eddie the pirate, my able seaman.

"All Aboard!" windows of the command bridge

Did you know?

Every ship's crew consists of various positions, serving in the different departments: The deck department, the engine department, and the catering (stewards') department. The deck department's responsibility is mainly to the ship's navigation, the engine department is mainly responsible for the ship's propulsion, and the stewards' department's main responsibility includes food and housekeeping. The officer ranks in the deck department are:
cadet (apprentice officer),
a third officer and a second officer, who are the navigation watch keeping officers;
first officer, who is the senior deck officer in charge of deck workers, operation of the ship, and the ship's stability,
and the **captain**, (**the Master**) who is the commander of the ship and responsible for it and for the entire crew.

cadet | third officer | second officer | first officer | captain

Port 2 – Limassol, Cyprus - 33°42'E

"So, tell me, Adi, the port from which we just sailed from – what's it called?" Eddie asked me a few minutes later.

I looked at him in wonder. "It's the port of Haifa. That's one of Israel's home ports. In fact, every country bordering the sea, has a port that is the naval gate to other countries around the world."

"Perfectly clear," Eddie answered. "And say, **this boat**... Where is she sailing?"

I laughed. "It's not a boat, **it's a ship, it's a Cargo Ship**, made of steel. Its length is about two hundred and fifty meters, and it's loaded with one thousand eight hundred and fifty-two containers, which we shall have to discharge on twenty-five different ports."

"Ah, of course", Eddie said, and then casually looked through the bridge window with a set of binoculars.

I smiled to myself. Eddie still had a lot of learning to do in the maritime field, during our upcoming voyage. How on earth did he get appointed to be my able seaman, without knowing anything about the different types of ships, ports, and the oceans.

But this was the case, and so, I decided to start teaching him all I knew from scratch.

"Did you know, Eddie, that the sea covers **70%** of the face of the earth? Various types of boats and ships sail through nautical routes, carrying versatile goods. In fact, most of the world's goods are transported by sea. Thanks to these ships we can all enjoy a life full of abundance.

This is how we get our clothes, furniture, rice, fish, eggs, toys, computers, cars, and many other commodities. As a matter of fact, **most goods and international transportation travel by sea, even in the 21st century**, despite the massive development of transport means, by air and by land."

"Oh, all this is perfectly clear," Eddie said while approaching me, "and say, this boat of ours – it's sailing east, isn't it?"

I sat down on the seat by the steering wheel and sighed.

70%

"We're on a **ship**, Eddie, not a boat, and it's sailing **westwards**. You are familiar with the Compass Rose, right?"

"Hmmm... I might have fallen asleep during that class... Could you remind me what it was all about, if it's no bother, of course."

"Gladly. The Compass Rose is a map that displays the orientation of the cardinal directions: north, south, east, and west. You can also see the intermediate directions north-east, south-east, south-west and north-west."

"Oh... that Compass Rose..." Eddie interrupted me, "And we are now sailing right into the Indian Ocean, to import clothes from China... Don't say a word, I'm on it!"

I cleared my throat. "Hmmm... not exactly. We're sailing in the Mediterranean towards Italy, where we will unload goods and load shoes, which will be imported to Israel."

Compass Rose

Quiz — I sailed to visit Yosemite National Park. Where am I?

Where do they come from?

The furniture is from Sweden, The TV from Japan, The health snacks from Mombasa, The flip-flops from Brazil, and the electric cars from America.

"You do know the different oceans and various continents, right?" I tried my luck again.

"Continents and oceans – Sure, I can recognize them like the palm of my left hand!"

Only then did I realize that little Eddie didn't have a proper hand, but an ironed hook instead. I decided to ask him about it later. Meanwhile I hurried to save him from another embarrassment. "The Pacific Ocean, the Indian Ocean, the Atlantic Ocean, the Arctic Ocean, and the Southern Ocean. The continents: Africa, Asia, America, Australia, Europe and..."

"And Antarctica," Eddie called, "Our ice breaker ship is on its way to break through huge glaciers, as we speak. For your information, Third Officer Adi, this was my best subject, I was even first in my class." Eddie straightened and puffed out his small chest.

I half smiled. "Boats and ships differ from each other according to their size and professional character."

Boats are generally vessels intended for navigation of coastal and inland waters. They usually weigh under 500 tonnes, use simple equipment, have simple constructions and designs, and their crew is mostly uncertified.

For example:

A wooden boat with oars

An aluminum motorboat

A rubber motorboat

An ancient sailing ship

A luxury motorboat

A luxury motorsailer

Ships are ocean going vessels, that operate in oceanic zones and high seas. They usually weigh more than 500 tonnes, have complex equipment, their crew members are certified engineers and deck officers, and their structure and design is complicated.

For example:

A wide variety of ships has been built and developed throughout history. To this day ships of various types are built from different materials, for example, wood, plastic, and metal. In the past ships were powered by sails and oars, and each ship loaded different types and sizes of cargo on board.
The first boats in the world were made of wood.

For more information regarding vessel types, scan QR and enter IMO site. (the International Maritime Organization)

A container ship

A cruise ship

Ships have accompanied us since the beginning of humanity and are our basis for technological and cultural development. They have always been used for discovering continents, for international trade between countries, for fishing, for food, for warfare, and for the defense of countries, for moving between countries, (immigration), and for travel and pleasure. From a political point of view, the existence of ship fleets, such as a merchant fleet, a war fleet, or a fishing fleet, is crucial for the existence of countries themselves, and for the economic and cultural development of the entire world.

The Great Britain Ship is a 19th century passenger ship

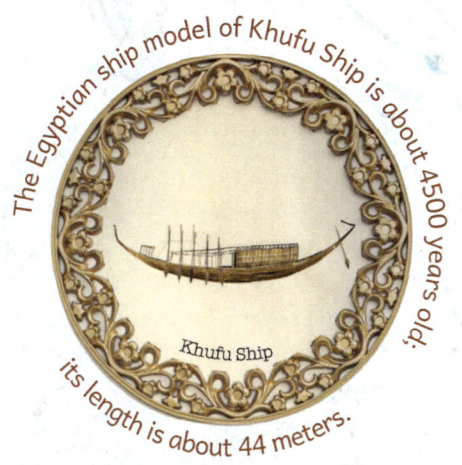

The Egyptian ship model of Khufu Ship is about 4500 years old; its length is about 44 meters.

A Moment in history

The main means of transportation, in which people traveled from country to country and from continent to continent was by ship. Ellis Island is an example of an immigration station in New York Harbour. In fact, 40% of Americans are descended from immigrants that came through this station, which opened in 1892.

scan QR

scan QR

Further information regarding Immigrants at Ellis Island you can find on YouTube #historychannel

Suddenly a call was heard on the communication system:

"Watch Keeping Officer Adi, reduce speed to five knots for lifeboats drill."

Eddie jumped from his seat. "What happened? Why five knots? Weren't the loads tied up well enough?"

I laughed out loud. "You really did doze off in quite a few classes... Come on, Eddie, how do you measure sea sailing speed?!"

I noticed Eddie was turning pale and hurried to bail him out again. "The speed of driving cars is measured in kilometers or miles per hour, while in marine vessels, the term **"knot"** or **"nautical knot" is used to measure speed at sea.**"

"Ah, yes," Eddie nodded vigorously, "like a knot in a rope, right?"

"Yes, the maritime speed unit is named after the ancient method of measuring the speed of ships and is accepted as a unit of speed at sea and in the air. One knot equals 1 nautical mile per hour, **which means approximately 1.852 kilometers per hour.**"

More about a simple marine speedometer (chip log) is attached to this Wikipedia link.

Eddie rose from his seat in the luxurious bridge console and started tracing back and forth.

"Hmmm... you know, it's been a long time since I put something tasty in my barrel..." he started patting his stomach. "Where do you grab something to eat around here?"

"In the hull of the ship, in the Mess on the first floor, there's a kitchen and a dining room for all crew members, you can go and ask the cook for something to eat," I answered and lowered the cruise speed.

"Hmmm... and this Mess .... it sounds like a real mess; how exactly do I get there?" Eddie looked more confused than ever.

"Look," I took out a piece of paper and quickly scribbled all the parts of the ship on it, then handed it to him.

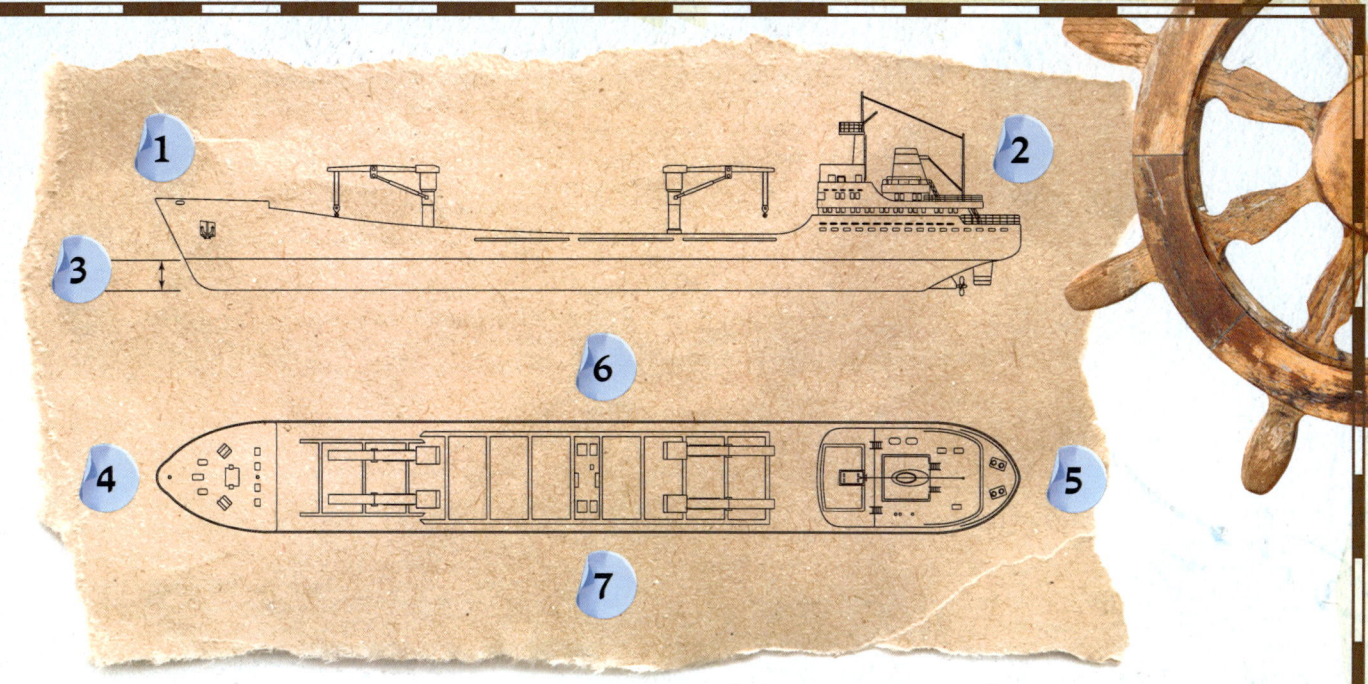

1. **Bow** - the foremost part of the vessel
2. **Stern** – the back part of the vessel
3. **Draft** - the distance between the surface of the water and the bottom of the vessel, namely, the depth at which the vessel sinks below the surface of the water
4. **Forward** - towards the direction of the bow
5. **Aft** - towards the direction of the stern
6. **Starboard Side** - the right side of the vessel
7. **Port Side** – the left side of the vessel

Eddie turned the page from side to side. **"But where exactly am I now?"** he asked almost in a whisper.

I took out another piece of paper, drew an illustration of the ship and noted all its parts. "Take it," I said, "now there's not a chance you'll get lost."

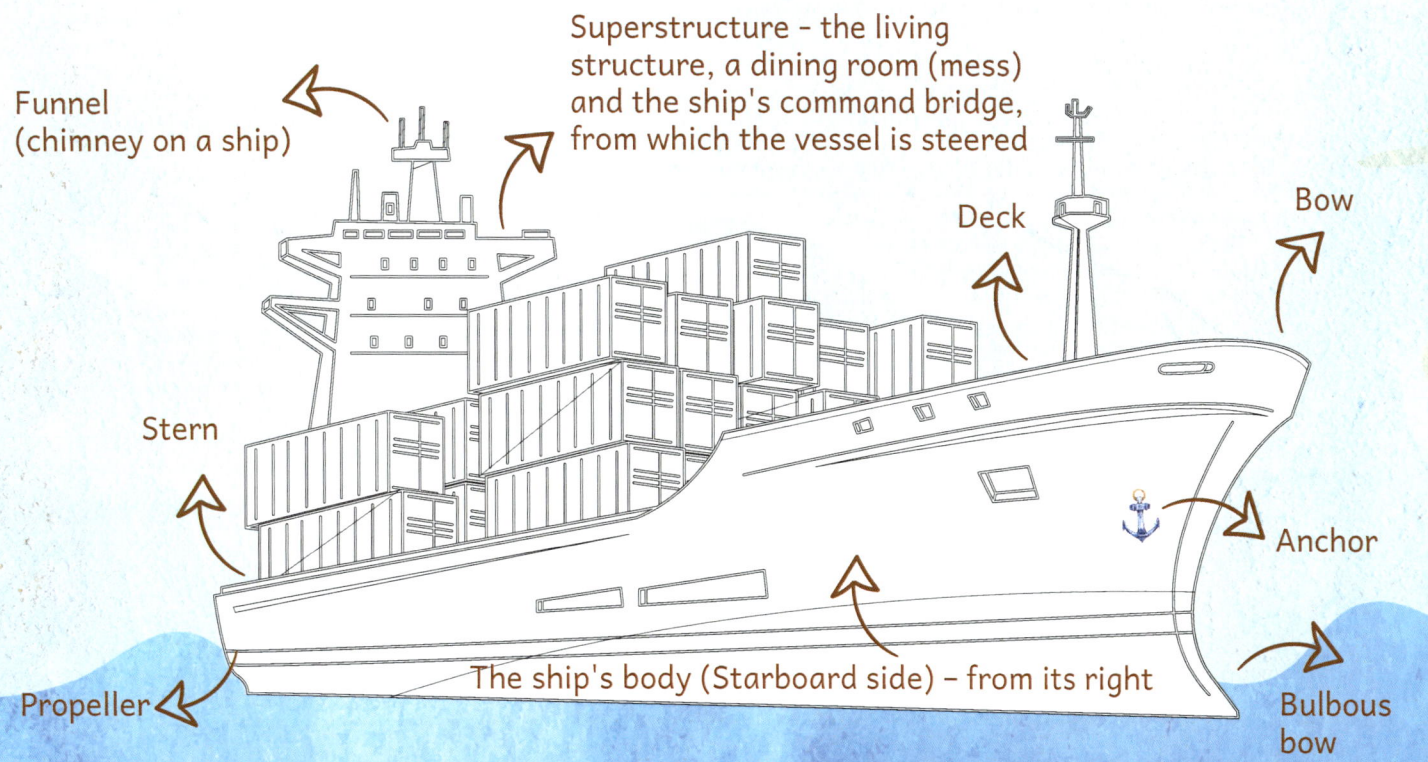

Port 5 - Thessaloniki, Greece - 22°56'E

About two hours later Eddie returned from his wanderings aboard the ship, holding a small map of the world in his hand.

"I got it from a sailor from Senegal," he said excitedly. "He arrived at Haifa port on a ship from India. When I asked him how he sailed all the way from India, he said he passed through the Suez Canal. Look, he must have passed here!" Eddie said excitedly and handed me the map in his hands.

"Wonderful!" I exclaimed, "come on, let's go."

Together we made our way to the Chart Room behind us.

"Look, on the sea routes around the world **there are sea crossings that are used for the passage of ships and the transport of goods.** These crossings significantly shorten the maritime routes for ships. Here, you will see some of the most important ones:

Watch ships crossing the Panama Canal in real time, on the official Panama Canal website link

scan QR

The Strait of Dover

The Panama Canal

scan QR

Watch a video which demonstrates the Panama Canal crossing at high speed on Radiofreebc Channel on You Tube

Quiz

On my way to Romania I crossed a strait. Which strait am I sailing through?

The **Panama Canal** connects the Atlantic Ocean to the Pacific Ocean;
The **Suez Canal** shortens the way from the Red Sea to the Mediterranean Sea;
The **Strait of Gibraltar** connects the Mediterranean Sea to the Atlantic Ocean;
The **Bosporus Strait** separates the European part of Turkey from the Asian part and connects the Sea of Marmara with the Black Sea.
The **Strait of Malacca** is the main shipping route between the Indian Ocean and the Pacific Ocean;
The **Strait of Dover** connects the North Sea with the British Channel and from there to the Atlantic Ocean;
The **Strait of Hormuz** connects the Gulf of Oman in the Indian Ocean with the Persian Gulf..."

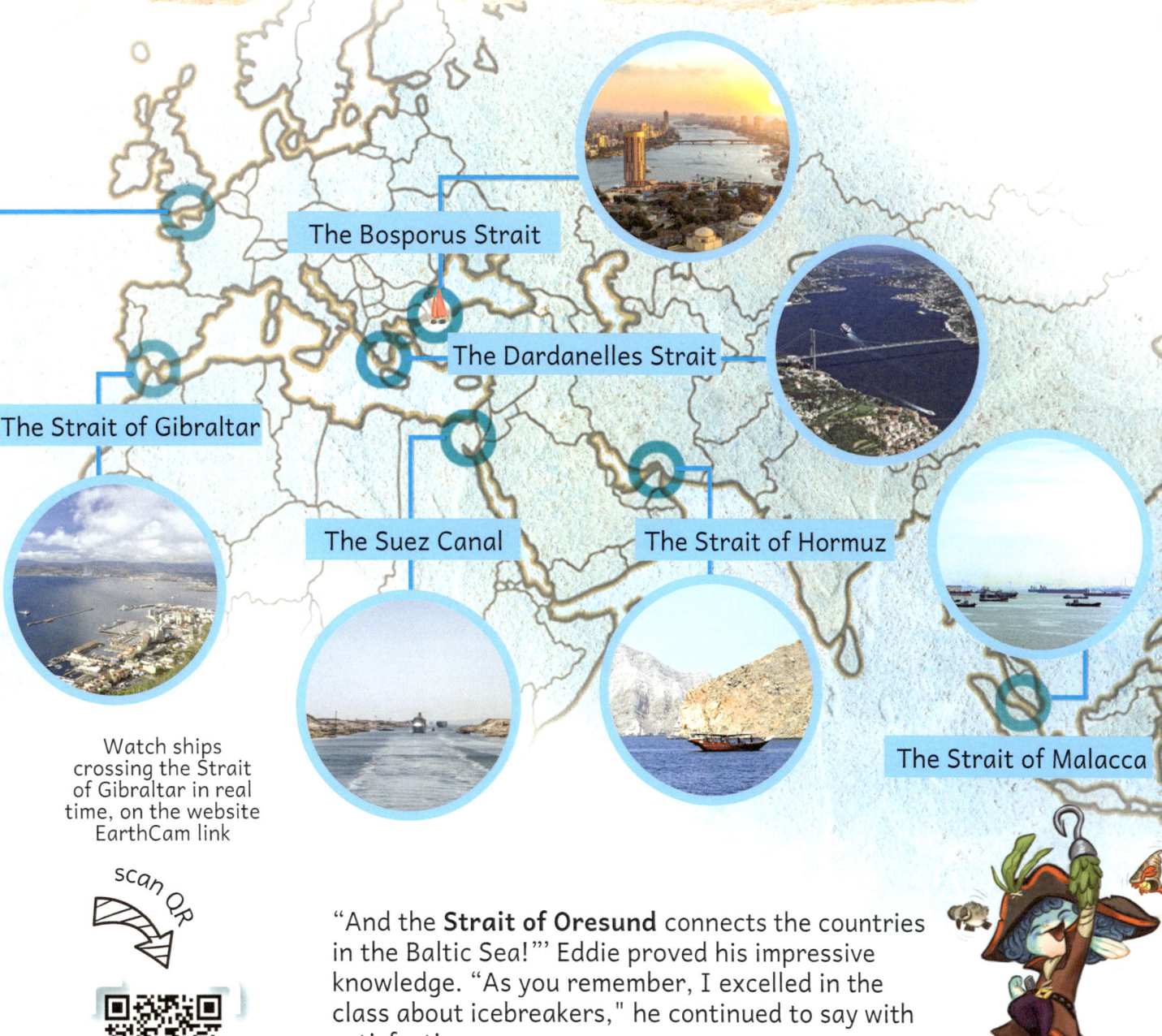

Watch ships crossing the Strait of Gibraltar in real time, on the website EarthCam link

scan QR

"And the **Strait of Oresund** connects the countries in the Baltic Sea!'" Eddie proved his impressive knowledge. "As you remember, I excelled in the class about icebreakers," he continued to say with satisfaction.

I laughed, "Even I myself didn't know that."

Port 6 – Napoli Italy - 14°18'E

Eddie enjoyed exploring the map in his hand, checking passages, and measuring distances between different countries.

"But tell me, if my ship wants to cross the Pacific Ocean from the West Coast of the United States to the East Coast of China - how long will we have to sail? A week?"

"Ha-ha," I laughed. "Such a voyage would take **seventeen days in a row**, Eddie, just like the route we're about to travel on the **Ocean 16**."

"Seventeen days!" Eddie cried. "That's a long time without seeing your family and friends," he sighed.

We continued sailing, and a few days later arrived at the port of Italy.

I navigated us to the discharging dock. With the completion of the ship's maneuvering and tying up, the operation of discharging cargo began.

The operators and port workers began to transport the containers which were at the bottom of the ship quickly and efficiently to the ships dock. Eddie stood on the deck and watched.

Map of sailing routes for ships in the Pacific Ocean

Seventeen days!

"This will never end!" he exclaimed. "These metal crates just keep on coming!"

"There are a lot of containers in the cargo holds of container ships, and if you look closely, you'll see that they are all the same size: about 12 meters long, 2.5 meters wide and about 2.5 meters high. Just about the size of an average living room at home."

"Yes, even bigger than the cabin we sleep in," Eddie murmured, "But what's in them?"

"**Container Ships** transport toys, books, computers, furniture, and everything that can fit inside them."

20 feet long — 8 feet wide — 8.6 feet high

scan QR

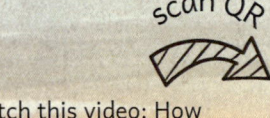

Watch this video: How a Steel Box Changed the World: A Brief History of Shipping, on 'Wall Street Journal Channel' on You Tube.

Packages and crates

Container Ship

Loading cargo in containers began in the 1950s, about seventy years ago, and from then on that's one of the main methods of transporting cargo. **The manufacturer packs the goods in packages and crates, which are loaded into the container**, these are transported to the ship, and from there to their destination.

All this is done without the need for repackaging, when loading on the ship. Today almost all non-bulk cargo is transported this way.

The volume of a container is measured in TEU units – Twenty-foot Equivalent Units. These units equal in size to the volume of a uniform container measuring 20 feet long (6.10 meters), 8 feet wide (2.44 meters), and 8 feet 6 inches high (2.59 meters), which is approximately 38.55 cubic meters.

"And what about bulk transfer?"
"Such as sugar, grains, rice, coal, metals..." I asked.
"How are these products transported?" Eddie continued to ask.
"In the huge cargo holds of Bulk Cargo ships or Bulk Carriers."

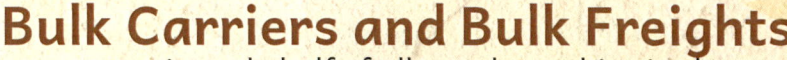

Bulk Carriers and Bulk Freights

are approximately half of all merchant ships in the world (about 40% of the number of ships in general).

These ships are different in size, starting with small ships, (with only one large cargo hold in the hull of the ship) to huge bulk carriers, carrying cargo weighing over 250,000 tonnes.

These ships are divided into several types, according to their unloading method.

Some can unload the cargo by themselves, and others depend on the cranes and offloading facilities in the port. There are also large bulk carriers, which can pack the cargo, while loading or unloading it.

These pictures display: **discharging cargo** - removing goods out of the ship's cargo holds, and **loading cargo** - putting goods into the ship's cargo holds.

Port 7 – Barcelona, Spain 2°10'E

A loud siren blew Eddie and me off our seats.

A huge ship was approaching the wide harbuor, with a large white crane on it.

"What's that? A whale?!" said Eddie, jumping beside me excitedly.

"It's a **General Cargo Ship**, or a **Freighter**. Notice that the cargo on the ship approaching us is packed in packages and boxes and is located on surfaces of different sizes. In the past, all commercial maritime traffic was carried out this way. Loading and discharging such a ship takes a long time and is very complex and complicated compared to the unloading of ships carrying other cargoes. This large white crane is designed to help unload and load the goods," I said as I pointed at the large crane.

A General Cargo Ship

Did you know?

The capacity in a General Cargo ship is calculated in volume units of a ton. The word **"Ton"** is derived from the old English word "Tun" unit of liquid volume (not weight), which means "a large barrel of wine". The Cargo Ship's capacity was specified by calculating the number of wine barrels the ship was able to carry.

We continued sailing west. While sailing along the coast of Spain, Eddie looked out at the harbour with a set of binoculars. "And what are those?" He asked, pointing towards a platform in the distance.

"These are **Heavy Lift / Cargo Ships**, designed to transport extremely large goods."

These ships are divided into two:

Ships capable of sinking in the water and loading other ships on them (e.g., warships) or other large marine cargoes, such as oil rigs, and transporting them to their destination.

The other type is **ships with heavy cranes on them**, that can transport large cargoes (for example, huge pipe parts or concrete), loading and unloading them in ports that don't have suitable loading and unloading equipment.

A heavy-lift ship transporting oil drilling rigs

Port 8 – Gibraltar, UKOTs - 5°21'W

When we were almost at the Strait of Gibraltar Eddie called out,

"Adi, look, it's a **Tanker**! **A Tanker carrying various liquids in the ship's large cargo tanks.** What do you think is in it? Oil? Chemicals? Refined products?"

I shrugged but was glad that Eddie had finally shown he had learned something in class.

"Hmm... I'm not sure. But it says it's powered by methanol, not fuel, so that's good news. Did you know that Tankers make up about 30% of the world's fleet, and their loading capacity reaches up to 300,000 tonnes, which is equivalent to approximately 2.5 million oil barrels?"

"I really hope there's grape juice in it," Eddie said and winked at me.

View of an Oil Tanker departing port and crossing the Atlantic Ocean (MSEA Capital Channel)

scan QR

Did you know?

Methanol can be used as an alternative fuel for ships. It is cleaner than regular fuel oil. Blue and Green Methanol can be produced from renewable resources. It's safe and easy to handle and available in ports all around the world. Clean Sea Transport, a pioneer in the clean fuel transition, took part in designing the first tanker ever with an engine that can run on both fuel oil and methanol.

More on Clean Sea Methanol Powered Vessels on this short video

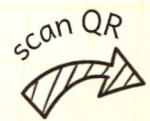 scan QR

CLEAN SEA
TRANSPORT

From afar I could see the narrow strait, where the two continents almost connected – Europe to the north, and Africa to the south.

"Look, Eddie, we're getting close to the Ocean."

Eddie jumped up and down excitedly, and the two sailors next to us on the bridge laughed. "Have we reached the Atlantic Ocean?"

"Yes, in a moment or two we'll cross the strait between the two continents, and then sail to the great sea..."

And indeed, a few minutes later we were greeted by the cries of seagulls in the distance. We started sailing through the waters of the Atlantic Ocean while A flock of dolphins and one whale rushed to swing their fins to the sides of the ship.

"What's that giant metal monster coming towards us?" Eddie asked, while looking out to the horizon.

"What do you mean?" I rushed to take the binoculars from him. A **RORO** Ship was approaching us.

Roll On / Roll Off Ships are used to transport cars, cargo on trucks and other cargoes on wheels, such as trailers.

They are called RORO (Roll on/Roll off ships) because the cargo is driven on and off the ship on its own wheels or using a platform vehicle, without the need for expensive installations, required on other cargo ships. Some RORO ships have a loading and unloading ramp in the bow and stern. These are inclined built-in ramps for the passage of cargo, which roll from the port floor into the holds of the ship and back, and as a result, shorten loading and unloading times.

Dangers at sea

We continued sailing in the open sea. At eight o'clock one evening, I went on duty, updating myself, as usual, on the state of the sea, the wind, waves, and visibility. The sea was as clear as a mirror, the stars shone in the sky and our ship made its way safely through the sea.

When the clocks on the bridge started to ring, I started my safety round, and then performed astronomical navigation exercises with Eddie.

"You see Eddie, that's the North Star, and this is the Big Bear..."

Suddenly, we were startled by a deafening alarm. We rushed to the Chart Room and to our astonishment heard beeping detectors and saw dozens of red lights beaming in the number three piston head area, in the engine room.

"**Oh no!**" Eddie cried.

"**BRAVO, BRAVO. BRAVO**, fire in the main engine!"

Our captain came running to the bridge and immediately took command. All the sailors and officers went on standby, while putting on their life jackets. The captain ordered to shut down the faulty engine immediatly, and so, all the engine pumps were turned off. The ship's crew began working on cooling the area and putting the fire out. Four hours later we could let out a sigh of relief, the fire was extinguished. I sat down on the navigation seat, exhausted. Now, when we were no longer in a state of emergency and continued our voyage westward, I recalled the lessons about dangers at sea, which I had learned: storms at sea, shipwrecks, collisions with icebergs, encounters with pirates, and... fires too.

Emergency drills on ships are very important for the safety of sailing, and for the personal safety of life at sea. Thanks to these regular exercises, in which all the crew members and passengers must participate, everyone knows how to act in the best possible way during an emergency.

The Nordic Empress - in June 2001, only four hours after leaving Hamilton port in Bermuda, a fire broke out at sea, due to a fuel pipe which had exploded and ignited in the engine. Thanks to the firefighting efforts, all the crew and passengers survived, and the ship was rescued, but had to return to Bermuda port for repairs.

The Titanic - the world-famous British passenger ship that sank after colliding with an iceberg in April 1912, during its maiden voyage from the port of Southampton to the port of New York. 712 people were saved and 1,514 people were perished in this disaster.

More stories from real survivers of the Titanic, watch British Pathé on You Tube

scan QR

Life jacket

Life buoy

Life boat

Port 10 - Hamilton, Bermuda - 64°46'W

"But wait a minute - where's Eddie?" I suddenly realized his absence.

I ran to the bow, and then all the way to the stern, went up and down the stairs, but I couldn't find him anywhere. The sky had started to clear and dawn broke... where could he be?

"A-hoy!" I suddenly heard a call from above me.

I looked up and saw him. He was standing on the "Monkey Island" above the bridge, where all the navigation antennas devices were placed. His right hand was pointing to the horizon.

"Third officer Adi, call all the crew to their firing positions, a warship is approaching us in high speed, we are in danger!"

I looked out at the horizon, and from a distance I could distinguish a large vessel approaching us quickly. Could this really be a warship in the middle of the Atlantic Ocean? I wondered.

I followed his finger with my gaze and could tell immediately that it was a tugboat, not a warship.

"Eddie, you can get off your position, it's just a **Tugboat**," I called out to him.

"A what boat?" Eddie called while stepping down to the deck.

"A Tugboat is a ship that pushes other ships and vessels or tows them with a towing cable. The Tugboat is very powerful, relative to its size. It must have a reinforced hull and a large and powerful engine, that takes up most of the space in the hull of the boat. Many tugboats are also equipped with firefighting equipment."

Monkey Island

Tugboats that sail in the open sea

There are three main types of tugboats:

1. **Tugboats that work inside the harbours** - their main function is to help various ships and large vessels in maneuvering at the entrance and departure of the port, as well as helping ships tie to the docks.

2. **Tugboats that sail in the open sea** - their role is to assist ships in distress that cannot navigate themselves, as well as rescue ships in danger, such as fire.

3. **Special tugboats that are designed for towing vessels without means of propulsion**, for example barges. They are usually used in rivers around the world.

Tugboats inside the harbours

Tugboats without means of propulsion

The days and nights passed pleasantly. When we arrived in Bermuda we spotted a Pleasure Ship, which resembled a huge hotel floating like a small village at sea.

"So, what do you say, Eddie? Would you like to take a vacation on such a **cruise ship**?

You could leave Miami, cruise to the Caribbeans, dock at the various ports, and then return to the ship, where you could splash around in the pool, or play mini golf, eat in fancy restaurants, go ice skating, or even spend time at the theatre, before you return to Miami..."

The world's largest Cruise Ship as of 2023

It rises to a **height of 72 meters** (the height of a 20-story building), it is **362 meters long** (the length of 20 buses), its **draft is 9.2 meters**, and it can carry 5518 passengers and **2200 crew members**, a total of **7718 passengers and crew members**. This is equivalent to the number of passengers in 15 Airbus A380 airplanes, or to the number of passengers in 150 buses.

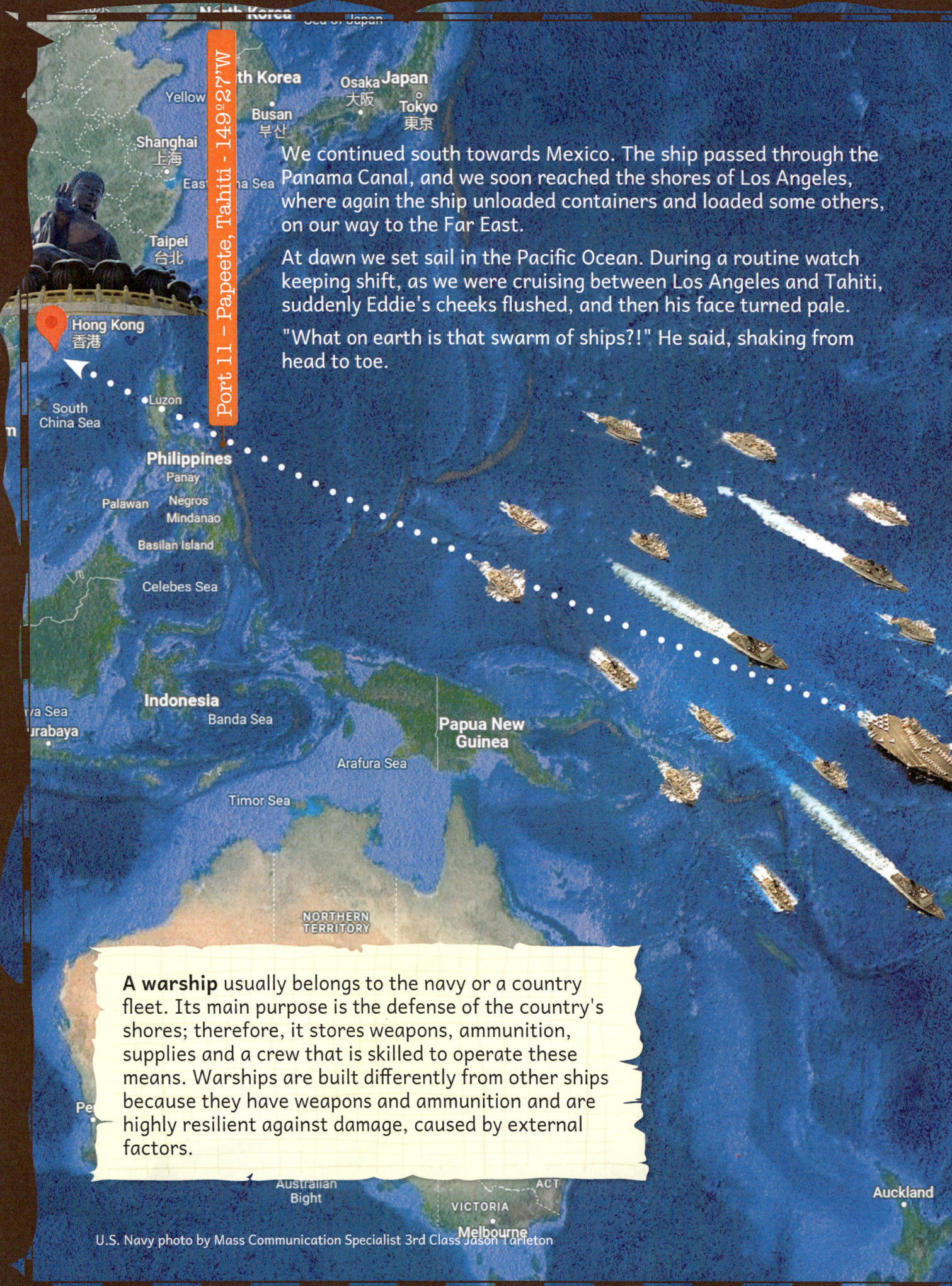

Port 11 – Papeete, Tahiti - 149°27'W

We continued south towards Mexico. The ship passed through the Panama Canal, and we soon reached the shores of Los Angeles, where again the ship unloaded containers and loaded some others, on our way to the Far East.

At dawn we set sail in the Pacific Ocean. During a routine watch keeping shift, as we were cruising between Los Angeles and Tahiti, suddenly Eddie's cheeks flushed, and then his face turned pale.

"What on earth is that swarm of ships?!" He said, shaking from head to toe.

A warship usually belongs to the navy or a country fleet. Its main purpose is the defense of the country's shores; therefore, it stores weapons, ammunition, supplies and a crew that is skilled to operate these means. Warships are built differently from other ships because they have weapons and ammunition and are highly resilient against damage, caused by external factors.

U.S. Navy photo by Mass Communication Specialist 3rd Class Jason Tarleton

I looked out towards the horizon. Sure enough, dozens of **warships** sailed before my eyes, but their face was not for battle.

"Don't worry, Eddie," I hurried to calm him down, "It's just an American navy warship drill, we're not in danger," I laughed and patted his shoulder gently.

"Oh, I knew that," Eddie chuckled in relief.

Days turned into nights, nights turned into days, and there was no stretch of land in sight. The crossing of the Pacific Ocean was long, and a sense of severe loneliness began to seep in. Our desire to get to land, to meet people and roam around the ports, was almost unbearable.

Until one morning a huge Buddha statue stood out in the horizon, observing us from the shores of Hong Kong. Fishing boats sailed from the coast towards our ship and back, carrying loads of treasures they had retrieved from the sea.

The sailing speed of warships is higher, and their navigation abilities are more sophisticated than those of ordinary merchant ships. There are various types of auxiliary vessels in a warship fleet, that assist the ships.

Their base is in the "mother ships" from where all the weapons depart, such as aircraft carriers, boats, destroyers and more. There are a lot of warship types, for example frigates, corvettes, missile ships, patrol and routine security ships, minesweepers, submarines and more.

Port 12 – Hong Kong, China – 114°10'E

Different Kinds of Fishing vessels

Various fishing vessels sailing all over the world are responsible for the supply of the fish we eat.

There are several types of boats and fishing vessels of different shapes and sizes. Some even hold fish factories, where the fish loads undergo a process of sorting, processing, packing, and freezing on board.

Did you know?

According to a study from 2020, the total number of vessels used for fishing in the world was estimated at approximately **4.1 million**.

After a short stay in the Hong Kong port, we set off again, this time to Taiwan and Korea. The sea was high, the waves washed over the deck, and our ship rocked from side to side. I looked at Eddie. This time his face was green. No doubt, he was suffering from seasickness.

Sea Sickness

Sea sickness is manifested by weakness, nausea and vomiting while sailing at sea. It occurs when someone is exposed to a movement pattern to which he's not used to. This is due to a contradiction between information which the brain receives through the visual system in charge of detecting movement, and between the equilibrium system, located in the inner ear. The equilibrium system of a person who is on a vessel sends the brain reports of shaking and vibration, while the visual system reports a state of immobility. As a result, discomfort is created, because the brain tries to "fix" this contradiction, and so the person may feel dizziness, nausea, weakness or vomiting. Seasickness affects everyone differently. Some people do not suffer from it at all.

Perhaps that is why this time Eddie didn't notice the danger lurking in the heart of the Chinese Sea. A pirate ship was sailing towards us quickly, and from a distance I could already distinguish the drawn weapons on its deck.

"Staff to firing positions!"

I immediately called out through the public announcement system, and within a short time, the entire crew assembled at their firing positions.

The pirate ship was getting closer and closer, and I feared the worst. **But then, a surprising turnaround occurred.**

The pirate ship changed its course and started sailing west. The weapons on it disappeared as if they hadn't been there at all, and I could see through my binoculars that some of the pirates were standing on deck and waving white handkerchiefs at us.

I don't know why, but I had a feeling Eddie was involved in all of this, and so I stepped outside the bridge.

And indeed, I soon noticed Eddie standing on the "Monkey Island", waving his drawn sword to the ship, which was already far off in the distance.

"Eddie, what are you doing up there?!" I called out.

Eddie jumped off and quickly climbed down from between the antennas. "Really, Adi, I'm surprised at you! Haven't you heard the tales about Eddie the pirate? I fought against all the pirates in the Chinese Sea. I am the world known champion of sword fights; I have won quite a few battles with only one hand! In fact, all the pirates in the Chinese Sea tremble with fear when they see me!"

"Wow!" I exclaimed, "so I guess you lost your left hand during one of those battles, did you?"

"Oh, this?" Eddie jumped on my shoulder, "No-no, I lost that hand in a battle with the red **mythological sea monster**... but that's a whole different story."

Pirates are naval criminals who have been infesting the international sea routes since the beginning of marine transport, and their goal is to rob the goods on cargo ships. Their main activity is in the Caribbean Sea, on the coasts of South and Central America, as well as on the coast of China and the Straits of Malacca, where they ambush merchant ships on their way to India, Africa, and Europe.

Port 13 – Alaska, U.S.A. – 150°W

Hours turned into days, the weather got colder, and in the distance, we could see the huge glaciers of Alaska and the polar bears in the Bering Sea.

While I was watching them, I spotted a ship which I knew would make Eddie extremely happy.

"Eddie, wake up!" I called out, while he was napping on the navigation bridge.

"I sincerely hope you have a good reason for waking me up," Eddie yawned loudly.

I nodded, and then let him see for himself.

"I can't believe it!" Eddie exclaimed and happily jumped up and down, "an Ice breaker! This is my dream come true!"

An **Ice breaker** is a ship intended to make way and navigate through ice-covered waters, as in the poles.

Did you know?

There are special travel companies around the world that specialize in organizing trips and cruises into Alaskan Gulfs, as well as trips to the North Pole. These tours include cruises on an ice breaker to the most northern point in the world and to Antarctica.

We started making our way back home. On the way we decided to stop at the busy and bustling Amsterdam port, to load different types of flowers and bring them to Israel.

The Port of Amsterdam in the Netherlands is one of the oldest and busiest ports in Europe. You can watch a complete and fascinating day - from sunrise to sunset - in which all possible types of boats and ships sail in and out of the port, on Drone Addicts You tube Channel.

scan QR

AMSTERDAM 38

We left Holland and headed home.

"See how suddenly our sailing speed increased without us doing anything?" I asked Eddie.

"How did that happen?" Eddie wondered.

"That's **the Gulf Stream**, of course! But don't worry, I'll use the automatic steering to overcome it."

"The what stream?" he asked in astonishment.

"Seriously? You slept all through the class about the ocean's currents too?" Nothing surprised me anymore. "Do you remember the turtles in the movie "Finding Nemo", how they used the East Australian stream to migrate from place to place?"

Eddie shook his head.

"Good, so now you have another important lesson to learn."

Port 14 – Amsterdam, Holland - 4°53'E

"When we swim in the sea, we feel underwater currents pulling us from the shore. These currents originate from winds, the continents' shapes and sizes, the water density in the seas and oceans, and more. Did you know that ocean currents can flow over thousands of miles? They have a great influence on the weather and climate in the continents bordering the ocean, where they are located. For example, the Gulf Stream, which is now flowing under our ship, makes northwestern Europe's climate much more pleasant than any other region on the same latitude."

"And what does all of this have to do with the automatic steering wheel you were talking about?" Eddie asked.

Sea currents flow regularly throughout the seas and oceans. There are also currents called Rip Currents that need to be considered when swimming near shorelines, because they can be dangerous, and may sweep swimmers deep into the sea.

In the Great Ocean Conveyor Belt drawing, you can see the large belt of currents in the oceans; in blue - salty and deep-sea currents, and in red - shallow and warm sea currents.

"**Marine currents** have a great influence on vessels. A ship sailing in an area where there are strong currents, must take them into account for navigation purposes, so as not to lose its way."

"So, all the animals we see in the water around us are related to the Gulf Stream?" Eddie asked.

"Yes, the marine animals hitch a ride on this current, to migrate from place to place."

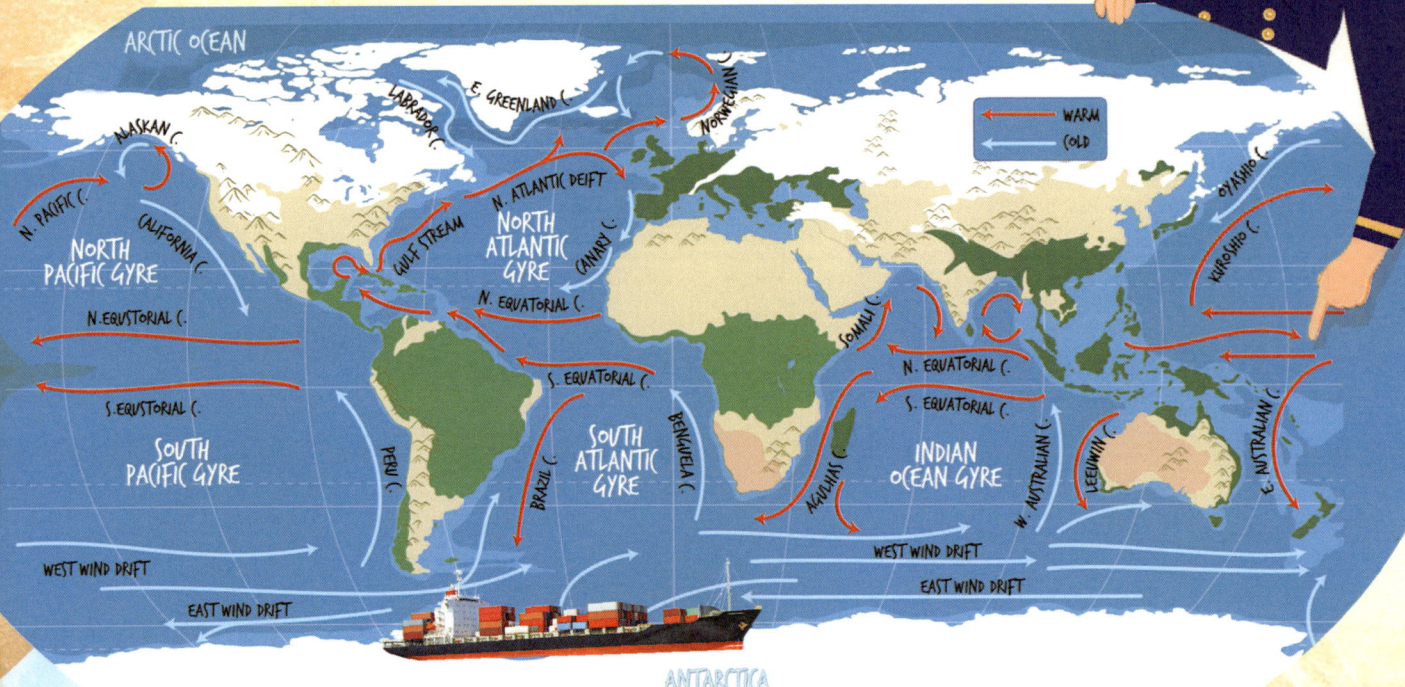

Along the way from the port of Amsterdam to the Strait of Gibraltar, I felt the influence of the West Winds (Westerlies), blowing from the west.

"Eddie," I asked him on one stormy evening, "You do know what goes on at sea at latitude 30° north, don't you?"

Eddi was busy messing with the instrument panel and pretended not to hear me.

"Ocean calling Eddie, ocean calling Eddie, can you hear?"

"Did you say something?" Eddie finally answered.

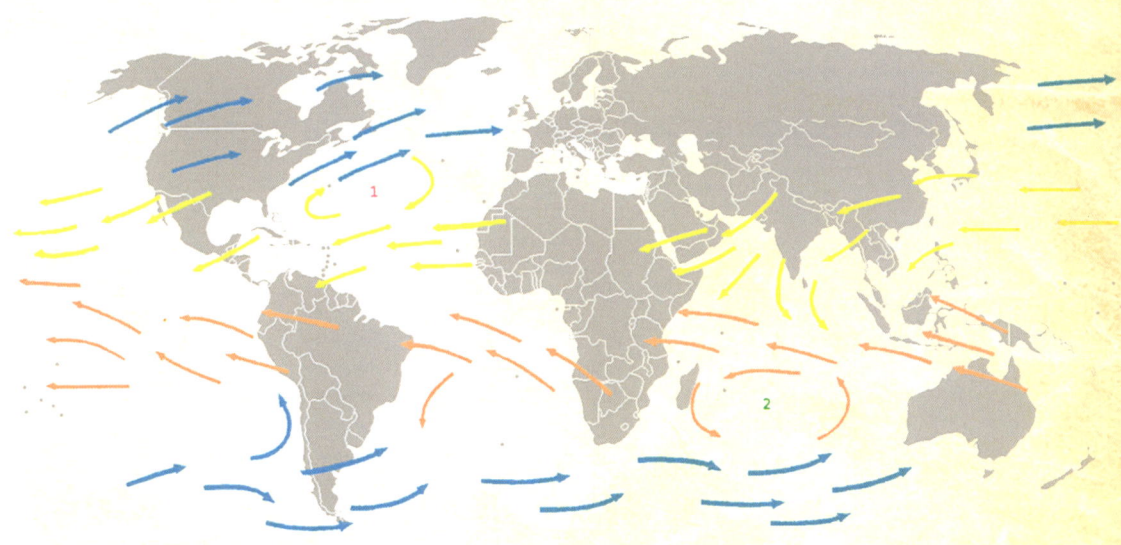

■■ The Trade Winds   ■ The Westerlies Winds

"I just wanted to refresh your memory about the Westerlies and the Trade Winds, the **constant stable winds** that blow on earth. The **Westerlies** blow from latitude 30° north and latitude 30° south, towards latitude 60° north and latitude 60° south. In the Northern hemisphere the winds are southwesterly, and in the Southern hemisphere they are Northwesterly.

The **Trade Winds** blow from latitude 30° north and from latitude 30° south towards the equator. In the Northern hemisphere the winds are northeasterly, and in the Southern hemisphere they are Southeasterly."

"Oh yes," Eddie was quick to reply, "You mean those west and trade winds..."

"And you probably also remember that they are called Trade Winds because the sailors who sailed the oceans knew how to use them as a driving force for their ships in their long commercial voyages. Thanks to their strength and stability, the Trade Winds made it possible to cross the great oceans in just a few weeks," I added.

Port 15 – Gibraltar, UKOTs - 5°21'W

We continued to sail towards the Strait of Gibraltar, facing east towards the home port of Haifa.

"Eddie, did you know **that at every given moment, you can look up almost anything about what's going on at sea and in different ports around the world?** Lots of information about countries, ships, boats, and other vessels is available on the network. For example: which ship sails to which country, what each ship carries in its cargo to its destination port, and what size and type it is. All you need to do is **open one of the marine sites, such as Marine Traffic, where you can find all ships, liners, buoys, and ports in the world, all in real time.**"

"But how?" Eddie looked confused.

"Look," I showed him,

"Just select a desired point/ship/buoy, click on it,

and all the information regarding that point will appear."

scan QR

pick a point

Cargo Vessel

right click

Position
Size
Departure
Destination
Goods

Port 16 – Haifa, Israel - 34°59'E

At dawn, after one hundred and five long days and nights, we finally arrived at our home port – Haifa. I couldn't help but get excited, when I noticed the lights twinkling at us from the Israeli coast. Our journey had come to an end.

After we were tied to the dock and all the containers were unloaded from the ship, Eddie woke up from his nap and jumped on to the instrument panel, then stood up in front of me and saluted with one hand.

"Well done, Third Officer Adi," he exclaimed excitedly, "It was a very good first voyage, I hope you learned a lot."

I gave him a wide smile. "Ay-Ay, **Able Seaman Eddie, thank you very much.**"

"I hope I managed to fill in some of your educational gaps," Eddie continued, "It seems to me that you doze off in quite a few classes over the years…"

Before my goodbyes, a **personal word** from me to you, dear girls and boys.

Our first voyage around the world may be over, yet the journey at sea and in life continues. New realms, fascinating ports and a sea of exciting experiences are always there to be discovered.

I encourage you to keep exploring and discovering the horizons and to widen your gaze far and beyond.

There's a big world out there. Anything is possible. Believe in yourself **and whatever you wish for** with all your heart, **you can achieve. Just dream it.**

See you on our next cruise.

With love,

Adi Elazari - Navigator on the path of light.

Thanks

The time has come to thank all those involved in making this book come alive – whoever helped, contributed, supported, and blew a gust of wind in its sails. If not for them, this voyage would have not come true.

Thanks to the **All-mighty Creator** of this World, for giving me the strength and courage, after seven years of writing and rewriting, to fulfill this task and successfully publish **Discover the Horizon**.

Thanks to **Tamara Avner**, the editor and translator of this book. Due to her, the informative sailing stories were given a life of their own and came together in an immersive and entertaining plot, full of experiences. Thanks for an attentive ear and your willingness to understand the ocean's story.

Thanks to **Gili Nativ**, my talented designer, a creator of magic. Your tremendous creativity enabled you to bring to life all that I had imagined.

Thanks to **Itay Levi**, my perceptive illustrator, who knew how to illustrate Eddie's character, with great imagination and a talented hand.

Thanks to my friends, the professional consultants in the maritime field, **Captain Dror Fern** from Israel, **Navel Building Engineer Martin Tomic** from Croatia, **Watch Keeping Officer Sivan Earon** from Israel, and **Mrs. Hagit Galatzer** from Israel, for their great ideas, attentiveness, and accuracy in everything related to seamanship.

Thanks to **Mr. Modi Mano, founder of MSEA CAPITAL**, for the cooperation and professional advice in the field of tankers in general, and for enlightening me with the knowledge of tankers powered by alternative fuels, and in particular innovative methanol engines.

Thanks to **Lior Biran** and **Karen Zaslavsky** for keeping me sane in a sea of storms.

Thanks to **Zelig and Batya Landsman**, my parents, who had to read and re-read different variations of my manuscript, who advised me and were there throughout our years together, while this book came to life. Thank you for your insights, for your queries, and especially for your generous support, only loving parents can give.

Thanks to my beloved family, **Hai Haim, Agam Shoshan, Maayan Stela and Peleg Yosef Elazari,** for always being with me in my heart and soul aboard our mutual ship, and for holding on together throughout this special voyage.

A special thanks to you, my **readers**, for reaching this page with me.

Would you like to broaden your horizons?

If so, please enter the **Maritime Professional** site, and countless other maritime sites around the world.

Links for enrichment

New York, New York USA

For more information regarding vessel types enter IMO site.

(the International Maritime Organization)

https://www.imo.org/en/OurWork/Safety/Pages/RegulationsDefault.aspx

More stories from real survivers of the Titanic, watch British Pathé on You Tube - https://youtu.be/_xKDRmhp6lQ

San Francisco, California USA

Further information regarding Immigrants at Ellis Island find on YouTube #historychannel

https://youtu.be/bDNKHWzQiz8

Watch a video which demonstrates the Panama Canal crossing at high speed on Radiofreebc Channel on You Tube

https://www.youtube.com/watch?v=-vi19z4LEi0

More about a simple marine speedometer (chip log) is attached to this Wikipedia link.

https://en.wikipedia.org/wiki/Chip_log

Watch ships crossing the Panama Canal in real time, on the official Panama Canal website link

https://multimedia.panama-canal.com/Webcams/miraflores.html

The big buddha, Hong Kong

Watch ships crossing the Strait of Gibraltar in real time, on the website EarthCam link

https://www.earthcam.com/world/spain/ceuta/?cam=gibraltar

Acropolis, Athens, Greece

More on Clean Sea Methanol Powered Vessels on this short video

https://mseacapital.com/clean-sea/

Marine Traffic, where you can find all ships, liners, buoys, and ports in the world, all in real time

https://www.marinetraffic.com/en/ais/home/centerx:-71.4/centery:9.8/zoom:2

Akashi, Japan

View of an Oil Tanker departing port and crossing the Atlantic Ocean (MSEA Capital Channel)

https://www.youtube.com/watch?v=Cjt06kT8GZ8

Would you like to broaden your horizons?

Enter the Maritime Professional site:

https://maritime-professionals.com/10-most-read-maritime-stories/

Watch a complete and fascinating day, from sunrise to sunset in the Port of Amsterdam, on Drone Addicts You tube Channel

https://youtu.be/ePDoCPi06rk

Barcelona, Spain

Quiz

1. What is the length of a nautical mile?
a. 1500 meters
b. 1852 meters
c. 80,000 meters
d. 80 meters

2. What part of the ship is called the bow?
a. The ship's hull
b. The back of the ship
c. The kitchen area
d. The front of the ship

3. What kinds of cargo do Bulk Ships carry?
a. Animals
b. Passengers
c. They don't carry anything, they are pleasure cruises
d. Coal, metals, and grains

4. Which strait connects the Mediterranean Sea to the Atlantic Ocean?
a. The Suez Canal
b. The Strait of Gibraltar
c. The Strait of Hormuz
d. The Bosporus Strait

5. Where does the captain of the ship navigate his ship from?
a. The Bow
b. The Bridge
c. The cargo holds of the ship
d. He changes his position during the cruise

6. What precent of earth's surface is water?
a. 7%
b. 0.7%
c. 17%
d. 70%

7. Which port is the busiest port in Europe?
a. New York
b. Hong Kong
c. Amsterdam
d. Haifa

8. What are the names of the stable winds that blow on earth?
a. Westerlies winds and Trade winds
b. Northern winds
c. Horizontal east winds
d. Draughts

Answers: 1-b, 2-d, 3-d, 4-b, 5-b, 6-d, 7-c, 8-a

My sailing log

Adi Elazari
Discover the Horizon
A Nautical Encyclopedia for Children

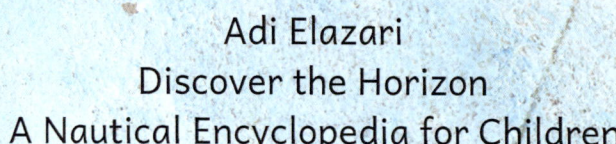

© 2023 All rights reserved to the author.
Translation from Hebrew, editing and linguistic editing – Tamara Avner
Graphic design and layout – Gili Nativ
Illustration of Eddie - Itay Levy
Credit photos - Shutterstock, Freepik

You may not reproduce, copy, photograph, record, translate, store in a database, transmit or otherwise receive any part of the material in this book. Commercial use of the material contained in this book is strictly prohibited except with the express written permission of the author.

ISBN: 978-965-598-722-5

1993-2006
Around the world photos
From an Officer's album
Adi Elazari

The sailor's prayer
"May we always sail on water
and never drink salty water"